For Sylvie.

Contents

Introduction
What Is Acting?

Acting isn't about pretending. It's about doing. In fact, the word "act" means: to do something on purpose. Actors don't fake it. They make it real.

Your job as an actor is simple...

- **Believe the make-believe.**

- **Make your fellow actors look good.**

If you can do that, you're already on your way to becoming a brilliant actor.

CHAPTER 1
What Do Actors Do?

An actor brings stories to life.

They do this by being characters in the story.

Characters are people, animals, or things the story is about.

The stories are written as scripts that tell the actor what the characters say and often what they do.

Actors take the words written in a script and turn them into emotions, actions, and connections with other actors. Sometimes they make the words up - that's called improvising.

Actors do this on a stage, they do it in front of cameras, and they do it from behind microphones.

CHAPTER 2
The First Job
Believe The Make-Believe

Let's say the scene you are acting in takes place on the moon.

Are you really on the moon?
No, of course not.

By using your whole body, voice and mind, can you believe it?
Yes!

With practice using their imagination, an actor can jump into any world at any moment - perhaps a castle, maybe a jungle or a haunted house - and believe they're really there.

Your imagination is like a muscle. The more you use it, the stronger it gets.

Athletes who train by lifting heavy weights all the time grow big muscles.

Actors who train by making believe all the time grow big imaginations.

Acting isn't pretending.

Acting is believing.

CHAPTER 3
The Second Job
Make Your Fellow Actors Look Good

You're never acting alone.

Even in a scene by yourself, there's an audience watching, reacting, and feeling with you.

Most of the time, actors work with other actors. That means your job is to support them and their job is to support you.

They support each other by:

Listening.

Reacting.

Giving each other what's needed to shine.

Actors are doers. They don't just say the lines - they believe what their character believes and do what their character does.

You're not pretending to be scared of a monster. You ARE scared because when you're acting, that monster exists for you.

And when the story ends, you stop acting and being scared because the monster no longer exists for you.

A few ways to be there for your fellow actors are:

- *If someone forgets a line, you keep the scene going. Help them recover - don't freeze.*

- *If a character needs a big emotional moment, feed them the energy to get there.*

- *If an actor's character is a queen - treat them like you'd treat a queen. If they are a bully, treat them like one, whether you're scared or standing up to them. Maybe both!*

Being part of a cast is like being in a team.

When everyone in the cast looks good, you look good.

CHAPTER 4
Acting Is Doing

The secret to acting is not acting. It's reacting.

You don't need fancy poses or big, over the top speeches, unless the script says so.

What you need is to know what your character wants and go after it.

If they want to win, do everything to win.

If they want to make someone laugh, do something funny.

If they want to be loved, show why they should be.

Every scene is about doing something, both with your feelings and your body.

Always ask yourself, what does my character want and what are they doing right now?

If the answer is nothing, then give them something to do, even if it's as simple as putting on shoes.

Even sitting still can be doing something if the character is waiting, hiding, or thinking.

That's acting.

CHAPTER 5
Where Can You Act?

You don't need to be in Hollywood to start acting.

You can act in:

- *School plays.*

- *Short films with friends.*

- *Audio stories or podcasts.*

- *TikTok and YouTube videos.*

- *Drama class.*

- *Theatre groups.*

- *Even reading books aloud with feeling!*

Every time you practice acting, you get better!

CHAPTER 6
Your Acting Toolbox

Builders, carpenters or any craftsperson use tools.

So do actors!

A carpenter uses chisels, saws, nails and hammers.

An actor uses things like:

- *Voice.*

- *Body.*

- *Imagination.*

Try the following exercises to sharpen those tools.

Voice

Say "hello."

Now say it loud.
Then soft.
Then squeaky.
Then shaky.
Now powerful.

Now say it as if you're scared.
Then excited.
Then as if you don't trust the person you are talking to.

Body

Look at yourself in the mirror.

Now squish your face.
Then stretch it out.
Then pull as many different faces as you can.

Now change the posture of your body.
Then hunch over.
Then stand up really straight.

Now move your whole body.
Then move it in ways you've never tried before.
Then move it fast.
Then move it slow.

Now stand as still as you can.
Just being you.

Imagination

Think about a time when you felt really happy.
Now when you were sad.
Then when you were surprised.

Can you remember how they feel?

Do you feel them again?

When you finish this exercise, you can let go of those feelings
and do something that makes you feel good.

Use Your Voice, Body and Imagination

Let's put it all together.

Walk across the room being an angry pirate.

Now walk across the room as a worried robot.

Then walk across the room through thick sticky mud that stinks!

There are many other things an actor could have in their toolbox like scripts and costumes.

What are some other things you could add to your toolbox to be a better actor?

Remember acting is a skill and skills get stronger the more you use them.

CHAPTER 7
What's An Audition Or Casting?

Most importantly, an audition is an opportunity to act.

An audition or casting is your chance to maybe get a part in a show - on stage or on camera - by showing directors and producers, the people who make shows, what you can do.

There are different types of auditions depending on what kind of acting you're doing.

Each is different, but they all have the same goal - to show who you are and how you bring a character to life.

In-Person Auditions

For a play or musical. These often happen in a theatre or rehearsal room. You perform your scene in front of the director and production team.

Self-Tapes

Self-tapes are usually for film or TV. These are auditions you record at home. You're given a script with a scene to practise, then you film yourself acting and send it to the producers and director.

Online Auditions

Online auditions are video calls where you act live over the internet. These could be for theatre or film and TV.

If you're asked to do a self-tape, here's how to do it well.

- *Make the self-tape in a quiet, well-lit space against a blank wall.*

- *Use a phone or tablet to film it. Make sure the camera is steady and level.*

- *Film in landscape (sideways) and not portrait, unless they say to.*

- *Make sure your face is clearly seen from the chest up, unless they ask for something different.*

- *Ask a parent, sibling, friend or someone else you trust to read the other lines if it's a scene with two characters.*

- *Speak clearly. Don't rush, and stay connected to the character.*

- *Watch the video before you send it. Make sure you're easy to hear and see.*

Whether it's a self-tape, an in-person audition or online casting, if you do the following you'll nail it.

- *Know what your character wants.*

- *Learn your lines.*

- *Stand still and strong. Don't fidget (unless the script says to).*

- *Breathe. Good actors are relaxed actors.*

- *Be kind to yourself.*

And if you don't get the part, that's okay.

It's always about what the directors and producers need for that character.

It's never that you weren't good enough.

You can't play every character. Every role won't suit you and that's okay. A character must be similar to you in some ways.

Great actors audition all the time and don't get chosen.

It's part of the job.

Eventually, you will get a role. If you keep trying.

So when auditioning or being cast, don't act to please the people watching.

Don't do what you think they want.

Just be you. Show them you as that character.

Be grateful for the chance to act, even if it's only for a short time in an audition.

CHAPTER 8
Butterflies Are Normal
How To Handle Nerves

Everyone gets nervous sometimes. It's normal to feel butterflies in your tummy before a show or an audition.

Being nervous means you care and that's a good thing.

The trick is to learn how to use that nervous energy to help.

Here are some ways to help with nerves:

- *Breathe slowly and deeply to calm your body and clear your mind.*

- *Focus on the character, not on people watching.*

- *Practice, practice, practice. The more you're prepared, the more confident you'll feel.*

- *Shake your body! Move, stretch, or jump up and down to release the nervous energy.*

- *Remember, the people watching want you to do well.*

Courage doesn't mean you have no fear.

It means you feel the fear and do it anyway.

CHAPTER 9
What's A Rehearsal?

Before a show, actors rehearse.

Rehearsing means practising what you do and say in the scenes over and over until everything feels right.

Rehearsals are where you:

- *Try new things.*

- *Learn your lines.*

- *Learn your movements, that's called blocking.*

- *Get better at being your character.*

- *Get direction from the director.*

- *Work with the other actors in the cast.*

To be a great actor means being a great team member by:

- *Getting to rehearsals on time.*

- *Being ready to work.*

- *Listening.*

Making mistakes in rehearsal is a good thing because that's how we learn.

CHAPTER 10
Your First Show

It's happened!

You auditioned, got a role, rehearsed, and now it's time to do your thing with the other actors for an audience for the first time.

What should you expect with your first show?

You might feel excited, scared, or both. That's okay!

You'll get ready in a dressing room or backstage area.

You'll have cues like music, lights or lines from other actors that tell you when to go on. You'll know these from the rehearsals.

You'll do your best and that's more than enough.

Remember to:

- *Support the other actors because you're in it together.*

- *If something goes wrong, keep going. The audience doesn't know what is supposed to happen, they will never know a mistake was made if you keep going.*

- *Take a bow at the end. Celebrate with your castmates and friends what you have all achieved.*

You did something amazing. Feel good about it!

CHAPTER 11
Your First Time On Camera

Acting for the camera is different from acting on stage but it's just as fun!

Here's how it's different:

- *You don't perform in front of an audience. You perform in front of a camera, maybe many cameras.*

- *Even though there's no audience watching, there are still people looking at you called the camera crew. They are all doing their own jobs to make a great film or TV show.*

- *The director will ask you to do the same scene many times with the camera in different spots.*

- *You'll need to hit your marks. Marks are tiny spots on the floor that show you where you need to stand. They also help the camera stay focused on you.*

- *What you do needs to be smaller, especially with your face. The camera picks up everything, even a twitchy eyebrow or too much blinking.*

- *You don't need to be loud, microphones can hear a whisper, but you still must speak clearly.*

Do the following to be a good screen actor:

- *Listen to direction from the director. Little changes make a big difference on screen.*

- *Be relaxed between takes. Remember, a good actor is a relaxed actor.*

- *Be patient. Filming can take a long time. You will spend more time waiting than you will acting.*

- *Never look at the camera when acting, unless the script or director says.*

- *Be truthful and keep it real, even with all the lights, microphones, crew and equipment around you.*

And remember, it will feel different, but your job is still the same.

Believe the make-believe.

Make your fellow actors look good.

Chapter 12
Quick Tips

Whether you're acting for the stage or screen, don't ever forget to:

- *Believe the world of the characters.*

- *Support your team.*

- *Listen with your whole body.*

- *Learn your lines.*

- *Take direction without taking it personally.*

- *Always keep learning.*

- *And most importantly, don't try to "act." Do it truthfully, the way you would.*

For Parents and Carers
A Note From The Author

Supporting a young actor is about encouragement, boundaries, and safe opportunities.

Here's how grown-ups can help:

- *Enrol the young actor in drama classes.*

- *Enrol them in singing and dance classes to develop control of their voice and body.*

- *Help them make short films or record themselves.*

- *Encourage storytelling, reading, and curiosity.*

- *Talk about what the characters feel, what the story means and empathy - what it would be like to be in someone else's shoes.*

- *Help them make self-tapes and prepare for auditions.*

- *Ensure auditions and opportunities are age-appropriate and safe.*

- *Remind them it's not about being famous. It's about loving the work and being an artist.*

Curtain Call

So, you want to be an actor?

You already are.

If you can believe in the world of the story,

and help your fellow actors shine,

you've got everything it takes.

Now go.

Do.

GLOSSARY
Acting Words And What They Mean

Actor: A person who plays a character in a story.

Action: The word a director says to start a take or performance.

Assistant Director (AD): The person who helps the director stay on schedule and keeps everything running smoothly.

Audition: A short performance you do to try to get a part in a show.

Background Action: When extras start moving in a scene to make the world feel real.

Beat: A pause or small moment in a scene that means something.

Blocking: The plan for where and how actors move in a scene.

Boom Mic: A microphone on a long pole that picks up sound while staying off camera.

Callback: A second audition when they want to see more from you.

Call Time: The time you need to arrive on set or at rehearsal.

Camera Assistant (AC): A crew member who helps the camera operator with focus, lenses, and equipment.

Camera Left/Camera Right: Directions from the camera's point of view, not the actor's.

Camera Operator: The person who works the camera during filming.

Cast: All the actors in a show.

Casting: Choosing which actors will play which characters.

Character: The person (or animal, or thing!) you are playing.

Choreographer: The person who creates and teaches dances or movement for a show.

Cinematographer/Director of Photography (DP): The person in charge of how everything looks on camera, including lighting and camera shots.

Close-Up: A camera shot that shows your face or a small detail.

Cold Read: Reading a script aloud for the first time without practice.

Composer: The person who writes the music for a show or film.

Costume: The clothes your character wears.

Costume Designer: The person who plans and creates what the actors wear.

Crew: The team behind the scenes (camera, lighting, sound, etc.).

Cue: A signal that tells you when to speak or move.

Cut: The word a director says to stop the action during filming.

Director: The person who helps guide the actors and shape the show.

Director's Note: A suggestion or change a director gives during rehearsal.

Downstage: The part of the stage closest to the audience.

Dolly: A wheeled platform that moves the camera smoothly during a scene.

Dresser: A person who helps actors change costumes quickly during a show.

Editor: The person who puts all the filmed scenes together into the final version of the film or episode.

Extra: An actor in the background who doesn't usually speak but helps make the world feel real.

Eye Line: The spot you're meant to look at so it looks right on camera.

Fight Choreographer: The person who plans safe stage fights and action scenes.

Fourth Wall: The imaginary wall between the actor and the audience.

Gaffer: The person in charge of lighting on a film set.

Grip: A crew member who sets up equipment like tripods and dollies to help move or hold the camera.

Hair and Makeup Artist: The person who styles your hair and does your makeup for your character.

House Manager: The person who looks after the audience and theatre space during a performance.

Improvisation (Improv): Making up your lines and actions without a script.

Lighting Designer: The person who plans the lighting for each scene or performance.

Lines: The words your character says in the script.

Mark: A spot on the floor where you stand so the camera can see you properly.

Microphone: A device that picks up sound. Sometimes clipped to your costume or held out of frame.

Monologue: A speech by one character, often alone.

Motivation: The reason your character does something.

Objective: What your character wants in a scene.

On Location: Filming in a real place, like a park, house, or street.

Pick-Up Shot: A small part of a scene filmed again to fix or improve something.

Playback: Watching or listening to the recording after a take.

Producer: The person who organises everything and helps pay for and manage the show or film.

Production Assistant (PA): A helper on a film or TV set who supports the crew with all kinds of jobs.

Production Designer: The person who designs the overall look of a film or play, including sets and props.

Props: Objects actors use during a scene (like books, phones, or cups).

Prop Master: The person who finds, organises, and takes care of all the props.

Rehearsal: Time spent practising the show before the performance.

Runner: Someone who delivers messages and helps move things around on set.

Scene Partner: The actor you share a scene with.

Screen Test: A filmed audition to see how an actor looks and sounds on camera.

Screenplay: The words and instructions written for a film or TV series.

Script: The words and instructions written for a play. Sometimes the word script is used for a film or TV series.

Self-Tape: A video audition you record and send in.

Set: The scenery and furniture used to show where the story takes place.

Set Designer: The person who creates how the set looks for a play or film.

Slate: A short introduction at the start of a self-tape or audition (your name, age, role).

Soundcheck: A test to make sure voices and sounds are being recorded clearly.

Sound Designer: The person who creates and mixes sound effects and background audio.

Stage Fright: Feeling nervous before performing. It happens to everyone!

Stage Left/Stage Right: The actor's left or right as they face the audience.

Stage Manager: The person who helps run the show smoothly and gives cues during the performance.

Stage Presence: The way an actor grabs attention and feels alive on stage.

Stand-In: A person who takes your place while lights or cameras are being set up.

Subtext: What a character is really feeling or thinking, even if they don't say it.

Take: A single recording of a scene during filming.

Table Read: When the cast reads the script out loud together for the first time.

Tableau: A frozen picture made by actors on stage.

Understudy: An actor who learns another actor's part in case they need to perform it.

Upstage: The part of the stage furthest from the audience.

Voiceover: A voice heard over the action, but the actor isn't seen speaking.

Wardrobe: Another word for the costumes worn in a film or play.

Wardrobe Supervisor: The person who manages costumes during a show or shoot.

Warm-Up: Activities that help your voice and body get ready to act.

Wide Shot: A camera shot that shows the whole scene or body.

Wrap: When filming or rehearsal is finished.

About The Author

Timothy Wilde is an award-winning writer, director, and drama teacher based in Australia. For over twenty-five years, he has helped hundreds of performers of all ages discover their passion for acting on stage and screen. He wrote this book because his nine-year-old niece, Sylvie, wanted to read something that could help her become a great actor. This book is for her - and for every young performer ready to take their first step on stage or in front of a camera.

About The Illustrator

Courtney Cottle is an Australian artist, actor, filmmaker, and illustrator whose work is driven by a deep engagement with storytelling across disciplines. A student of the author, she brings a performer's sensitivity and a filmmaker's eye to her visual work, grounding each illustration in character, emotion, and intention. In this book, Courtney's hand-drawn illustrations reflect the joy, vulnerability, and imagination at the heart of performance, helping young readers connect emotionally with the ideas on the page.

www.ingramcontent.com/pod-product-compliance
Lightning Source LLC
Chambersburg PA
CBHW042132080426
42735CB00005B/148